Faces of Wendell

An Oral History Project

For all the Wendellites
who have been and all to come.

Published by Human Error Publishing

www.humanerrorpublishing.com
paul@humanerrorpublishing.com

ISBN: 978-1-948521-76-5

Cover design:
Human Error Publishing
and
Ruth Flohr and Mez Ziemba

Cover photographs: Ted Lewis, Christine Heard, Dorth-ee, William "Boo" Pearson, Annie Diemand, Phyllis Lawrence & Jim Slavas, Susan von Ranson, Jonathan von Ranson, Rick Drohen, Nancy Spittle, Wendell Senior Center.

Photographs by Ruth Flohr

Back cover photo by Genevieve Gaignard

**"Stories create community,
enable us to see through the eyes of other
people, and open us to the claims of others."**

-Peter Forbes, photographer and author

Wendell's Two Room School House
Photograph courtesy of Harry and Del Williston

Faces of Wendell:
An Oral History Project
Book One

Thanks to Mez, Ruth and the high school interviewers
for putting together this thoughtful tribute to the hardy,
adventurous, countercultural and community-minded
souls who arrived in Wendell - 200 years after its first
intrepid settlers - and created a home, in every sense
of the word, for themselves and their neighbors. For
some, the stories and photographs in these pages will stir
memories and evoke nostalgia; for others, they will elicit
wonder, respect and maybe even emulation. Faces of
Wendell is a treasure for both present and future generations of this "magical" town.

- Pamela A. Richardson, author of *Wendell, Massachusetts: Its Settlers and Citizenry, 1732-1900*

I've had a love affair with Wendell for years and years,
so these stories are way more than interesting. I wish
that each were its own entire book. How fascinating can
a town get? And how does a town manage to retain its
character as a true, and a unique community? I suppose
that's what led to the impetus for this book. And yet it
still leaves me amazed and so grateful. I remember when
Wendell did its "places of the heart" project, which I
wrote about for The Recorder. It turns out that Wendell
truly IS heart.

- Richie Davis, author of *Inner Landscapes: True Tales
from Extraordinary Lives Goodwill & Ice Cream: More
Tales from Extraordinary Lives*

Contents

Dedicated to a Wendell Original

TED LEWIS w/Susie

10/10/1929 - 6/10/2021

Dedicated to our dear friend

Dvora Cohen

10/7/1953 - 1/11/2021

For Dvora
By
Mez Ziemba

meditation one

you are not
here
you are everywhere
your beautiful angel wings
are crafted
with pansy petals
every imaginable
shade of purple
your breath
has become
the wind
transforming
into the hummingbird's wings
as it hovers above the cardinal red
bee balm
bergamot
you are not here
you are everywhere

photo by Ruth Flohr

Preface

Our book Faces of Wendell began from our shared dream to capture the heart of Wendell as experienced and sustained through the people who have lived here. We both believed our unique community to be knitted together through hard work, open-minds, resilience, healthy differences, and love. We both had also experienced what some people around here call the "magic of Wendell" - the thing that causes some locals to say, "As soon as I got here, I knew this was my home." We had both felt the "magic" but couldn't quite put our fingers on it. In our own ways we each came to the conclusion that the only way to fully understand the heart of Wendell was to hear and preserve the stories of the people that have made and continue to make Wendell a family.

Like all family stories this one goes way back and is full of layers and nooks and crannies. We knew early on our book would become a series of books with stories beginning in the early 20th century until the present. Author Pamela A. Richardson had fortunately already dived into to the early Wendell days with her wonderful book, *Wendell, Massachusetts: Its Settlers and Citizenry, 1752-1900*. Pam's book draws largely on documents entitled "Materials for a History of Wendell" written by Wendell resident Thomas E. Sawin between 1843 and 1863. This history, told from one man's perspective along with Pam's meticulous research, is a gift. We hope to continue that gift with *Faces of Wendell*, sharing as many perspectives as we can gather.

Faces of Wendell took many years to arrive in print as it took many years for us to raise our young families and to gather the tools we would need to take on such a large project and to gain the trust of Wendell residents to tell us their stories. Mez did so by immersion - staying here since her arrival in the 80's and Ruth by leaving in the 80's to pursue her education, first at Smith College, then at San Francisco State University, and eventually returning in 2016.

The Back Story

Mez

I arrived in this beautiful town of Wendell in 1983 after living in the woods of Leverett and Shutesbury several times around, searching for the right piece of land. My son Jesse was 18 months old and I was pregnant with Christopher.

We bought a four acre parcel of land for $5,100.00 on what the locals called "The Plain Road". We were ecstatic to find a pristine piece of land across the road from a stream and wild life sanctuary. We used our tax return that year to pay for it.

The resident hunters however, were none too happy as it was where they had harvested deer for several generations before we came. We made friends and all was well. We cleared the land tree by tree while living in a trailer not fit for chickens. The trailer was heated by our homemade wood stove named "Piggy". We also put in a driveway and I planted sunflowers in front of the trailer. It was home.

Christopher was born and Jesse two years old when our post and beam house started to take shape. Our new salt box home was built with timber from the huge pines we had sent to Kicsza Lumber. For the first few months we lived with no running water, no electricity and no telephone. Our bathroom was a legitimate outhouse. Later Rupert Goddard from the center of town dowsed our land, found a vein and on a very rainy day our deep well went in. Vermont National Bank lent us the money and for a payment of $71.00 a month we had water! I don't remember those days being hard at all. It was an adventure and I was writing my own story. I was a modern day pioneer woman!

Mez with sons
Jesse Davis
and
Christopher Davis

We were fortunate to have family and friends who helped us build the house. My brother Mark and my dad Eddie came to work on our house as did Myles's brothers Bud and Matthew and their dad Jack. My mom, Joan and Myles's mom, Pauline nourished and supported us in so many ways. We basically lived by the seat of our pants but it worked out. Family is everything.

After the house was built I was elected to the Board of Library Trustees and started get to know the townsfolk. The library at that time was inside the building that's now our Senior Center.

My sons attended Pre-School in the building where our beautiful Wendell Free Library now stands. I taught there as well, getting to know other young families in town. In spring we tapped the majestic maple trees that used to be around the building and boiled sap with the children. It was a magical time.

As time went on I joined various other committees in town. I volunteered with The Ladies Aide and got to know Elsie Diemand and Virginia Wheeler. We sponsored Halloween and Christmas parties for the youngsters at the town hall. It was good, old fashion fun! It

11

was at this time I began realizing how very rich Wendell was with several generations staying here near their families to raise their own children in this village of approximately 800 people and over 7,000 acres of state forest.

The years marched on, my sons were growing up and I joined many other committees in town, getting to know more and more of the fine people who dwelled here. Years later I am happy to say that my two grown sons both own land in Wendell. Our house on New Salem Road sits right in the middle of their properties, one mile going each way.

It was at an Old Home Day celebration about five years ago that I had an aha! moment and the kernel, or seed of Faces of Wendell was born. I wanted to capture the essence of this special town where I had raised my children. This town of Wendell where I lived and felt grateful for. I wanted to interview townspeople and record their stories. I was particularly interested in the people who had grown up here, who had settled here years ago. I wanted to gather and preserve their memories, so that they would stay alive as time marched on.

Around this time I reconnected with Ruth, an old friend who had moved back to Wendell. I joined her memoir writing group and our friendship and mutual love of the written language was reignited. I mentioned to Ruth that I wanted to write a book about the people of Wendell. I had already named it Faces of Wendell! She said, "When do we start?"

Ruth

When I bought a small house in Wendell on Farley Road I had no idea what to expect from this little hill town. It was when Lisa Aubin and Annie Diemand "the Wendell Welcome Wagon" showed up at my doorstep with a basket full of local goodies including Diemand eggs and a Wendell Post, that I began to realize this wasn't just any small New England town. I was pretty sure these curious young women were there to check out me and my young family as much as to welcome us. Both missions accomplished. I loved them both right away. I had no idea that Lisa who also lived on Farley Road, would become my lifelong friend and confidante. Or that when I returned to Wendell after moving away for nearly 30 years, we'd again be living on the same street - West Street this time.

It did not take long for the magic of Wendell to reveal itself. My first trek down to the Mormon Hollow swimming hole, reached by negotiating a barbed wire fence and by side-stepping cow pies on the sloped cow pasture, introduced me to the concept of neighborhood skinny dipping. As I sat awkwardly on the mossy rock edge in my bathing suit, struggling to keep my eyes on other people's eyes I felt a developing fondness for these free-spirited people about to become my friends.

As one who appreciates the traditional as well as the progressive, I was thrilled to discover how both not only coexisted here, but fed each other into a pool of shared visions, occasionally fractured and reimagined by an unlikely mix of very different minds. I also was immediately smitten with the Wendell State Forest which shares space with us. We lived at the base of Bear Mountain which our new friend Michael Mack told us was nick named Spider Mountain. One afternoon I discovered why when it looked like the mountain floor was moving and upon closer examination I saw that spiders, I don't dare imagine how many, were crawling down the mountain.

My daughters Alison and Stephanie still share favorite childhood memories of Swift River Elementary School, their woods behind the house, good friends, Christmas parties at the town hall, Old Home Day, sledding down the cow pasture hill, and swimming at Ruggles Pond.

While living on Farley Road I became fascinated with Wendell history. As I took American Studies courses at Greenfield Community College, Wendell became fodder for my studies. I hiked the woods behind our house discovering roughly marked graves and even an abandoned trailer. My curiosity for the stories behind these discoveries was unquenchable. I read anything about Wendell I could get my hands on. Wanting to share my enthusiasm for Wendell, I invited several students from the American Literature class I was taking, to hike up Bear Mountain. Inspired by the Transcendentalist writers we were studying, we spent that cool morning quietly writing and drawing. My dear professor, Phyllis Nahman kindly accepted the collection of our work in lieu of me having to write a paper. Atop Bear Mountain, I had just led my first writing group.

In the late 1980's I left Wendell to attend Smith College and after a few jobs locally, on to Berkeley, California where I did my graduate work at San Francisco State University. While attending SFSU I also ran a writing group and retreat called Women Who Run With Words. My work facilitating writing groups informed my graduate research which focused on the value of personal stories and dialogue in building and sustaining culture. After earning my masters in Communication Studies I taught at a local community college until offered a position in the Communication Studies Department at SFSU. Although I loved teaching there I always ached to get back to the Pioneer Valley. When that opportunity presented itself, I bought a house on Old Egypt Road in Shutesbury, packed up my dog, two cats and drove with my friend Karen Frye across the country. Little did I know that the love of my life and eventual husband Peter Waters lived on the other end of Old Egypt Road in Wendell. We decided I'd move into his house and so I found myself back where my dream of running writing groups and gathering stories all started - Wendell.

That's where this story started for me. As I reconnected with Wendell I was quickly reminded of what I loved about this community. People support each other in a way that allows everyone to be who they are. I found support from the Wendell Cultural Council, Friends of the Wendell Free Library, and The Wendell Free Library. Their support allowed me to revive my writing groups. My earliest group was a memoir group which included Johanna and Don Bartlett, Chris Queen, and Linda Lau. This group morphed into a creative writing group. Phyllis Lawrence and occasionally Lisa Aubin and Jerri Higgins joined. We've been writing together weekly for over five years.

Another memoir group turned into a group of women writers known as Chalice of Crones which included Morning Star Chenven, Nancy Spittle, Shelley Hines, Nan Riebschlaeger, Kai Jud, Ilina Singh, Sharon Tracy, and Mez Ziemba. Mez and I hit it off right away. I appreciated her energy, vibrant writing, and all the work she did in our community. I knew I wanted to work with her. Mez had a project in mind that just happened to match where my head was going. When Mez told me about her idea to collect Wendell stories and put them into a book called Faces of Wendell, I jumped on board. My two ideas were to start a writing group called Written in Stone to begin collecting Wendell stories and a second project where Wendell teens would interview and record Wendell seniors, followed by a presentation for the town. We were off and running and haven't stopped since. Rosie Heidkamp, the librarian at the time said she envisioned a town full of writers. To keep this dream going we're already gathering stories for the second *Faces of Wendell*.

Most of the stories in this book were written by the people who participated in the Teen/ Senior Oral History Project. The story of Ted Lewis is constructed from a three-hour interview we were fortunate to complete before he passed away. The interviews conducted by the teens are recorded and available on DVD.

15

Stories From the Heart of Wendell

TED LEWIS

Interviewed by Sally Houle

"Back in the old days when anybody had any trouble the Grange helped out. We all helped one another. The kids would help the men lugging boards. The women would bring meals to us. You go up and work like the devil!"
   -Ted

Ted Lewis: Story from Interview
Transcribed August 2, 2021 by Mez Ziemba

I moved to Wendell when I was three years old. My grandmother was already here at 66 West Street. My parents came from Eastport, Maine where they worked in the sardine factories. My father had a painting business when the depression hit in 1929.

When I was a kid, West Street was all open fields and pasture all the way to Emma Capaluzzo's place. I liked the farm land, open land. I remember the Fiske Farm on West Street, owned by Alvin Fiske, an old timer. There were saw mills at Fiske Pond and an ice house too. I think the Fiske Farm and Fiske Pond are the prettiest places in Wendell!

Back in the old days you had to grow all your own vegetables. And, my mother, she made bread all the time. I have good memories of picking blueberries on our farm.We saved the money we earned selling blueberries to buy our clothes at Sears and Roebuck and Montgomery Ward in Greenfield.

"Those were the good old days!"

In the 1940's we picked tobacco for thirty five cents an hour. We would catch a ride to South Deerfield. Everybody worked for nothing back then.

My wife, Marjorie Powling was born on West Street where Margo Culley and Kathy Swaim live now. Her brother was Merle Powling who married Gladys Harrington. Gladys was the Post Mistress in Wendell for many years right there in the middle of town where they lived.

Marjorie and I went to school together and in those early days we fought like brothers and sisters! She played basketball and I kept score. We graduated from New Salem Academy.

After graduation I joined the Navy because I was sick of cutting wood. We didn't have chainsaws back then. We cut all the wood by hand. When I came home I asked her (Marjorie) to go to the movies, and that was it! Marjorie (Girlie) and I got married in 1950. We had three children, Dennis (Pab), Debera, and Marjorie (Opie). We have four grandchildren, three girls and a boy.

Ted in the Navy

Marjorie and Ted

My impression of Wendell?

"Well...you don't live somewhere for eighty years and not say it's good."

I've been in government here for many years. I was on the Board of Assessors for 14 years. We worked hard. There was no revenue. I also served on the Wendell Select Board for 39 years. It was good if we could solve people's problems.

Our first Fire Department was in 1954.
Floyd Peck was our first Fire Chief.
Myron Gibbs, Roland Jean and Everett Ricketts were on the fire department as well back then.

Back in the old days if anybody had any trouble the Grange would help out.
We all helped one another. (When there was a fire and a house needed rebuilding) The kids would help the men lugging boards. The women would bring meals to us.
You go up and work like the devil! The kids would miss school to help.

I've met some good people here.
You were always welcome to come here (to our house).
The start of Old Home Days was in the 1930's when I was a kid. It was right around Memorial Day. The band would come up from Orange and play.

Mrs. Smith made wreaths from the laurel we picked. Each kid would fight to get a wreath to put in the cemetery.

After all the services were over the mothers would make the meal. Everything was done by hand. Then we had to get home to put the gardens in.

We watered by hand. We didn't have hoses back then. Farmers never had the day off.

We all worked together.

Ted's mother Inez Lewis with cow

PHYLLIS LAWRENCE AND JIM SLAVAS

Interviewed by Ava Chiodo

"Wendell being on the edge of college towns in the valley became a home for young adults with educated backgrounds but little money at the time. A place where Old New Englanders would come to coexist with youth looking to create a different world from their own upbringing where bureaucracy of building codes, etc. had not yet taken hold so made it possible to a" back to the woods land movement." The meeting of the young people was not always smooth - but eventually perhaps people came to recognize common ground in Yankee independence."
   -Phyllis

The Outhouse
By Phyllis Lawrence

The outhouse still sits, slightly tilted back as one side slips its way back into the earth. It still gazes down on the little run-off frog and salamander pond that reflects bits of sky, and lines of tree trunks, and tangles of forest understory.

The outhouse is missing a board or two now. Its tin roof is rusted with tiny pinpricks letting in raindrops on a stormy day. Truth be told, our outhouse never did have a door. I wonder if it felt resentment without the crescent moon adorning its sacred entry. But instead, it was open to everything and that has to be wonder-full.

It began as a two-seater. Jim chiseled and filed the wooden holes to be smooth and welcoming, even on those frosty days; a place to spend a little time, to contemplate and reflect and work out things. When Noah was old enough to use such accommodations a third, smaller, and lower seat was added at a right angle so conversations with a three-year-old then became part of its history.

When sick and on dark, cold winter nights the outhouse might be considered a terrible inconvenience. But how often do young children get to see the stars at night, and to be comfortable in the dark, and to feel the crackling cold in their nostrils with a moon shining down? So ... no regrets....but I admit....no returning to those times either!

I arrived on the scene around 1971 or 1972 , bringing my goat "Liffy" (named for the river Liffy in James Joyce's Ulysses) with me. Soon there were goat kids and milking to be done, farm cheese to be made.

Our first sheep came home in the back of an old Toyota pick-up. An agreeable stranger had picked Jim up hitch-hiking on his way home from visiting friends in Northern Vermont. Jim had convinced his new companion to go with him to pick up two Scottish Blackface sheep that he had purchased in one of those moments of inspiration because every farm needs some beautiful sheep to graze the green pastures. Pastures that only existed in Jim's mind.

The Scottish Blackface sheep were pretty wild at first but truly beautiful with their long fibers that reached almost to the ground, their black and white coloring, and their large curled horns that spiraled around the side of their Roman-nosed, regal faces. With no fencing in sight, along with no pasture, these new residents were tethered at first and fed leaves of hay. Jim would hunker down near them, leaning against a rock and tell them his dreams. I'm sure they were not that pleased with their new state of affairs. We could only assure them that things would get better. And eventually they did.

Jim had bought the land in 1969 for $3000 with the generous help of Charles Smith who loaned him half the cost. The first summer he lived in a tent until a tree fell on it. The land had been logged apparently before any logging regulations were mandated around here, and if you took a step five feet in any direction you were met by a weave of criss-crossing of downed tree tops.

It was ankle turning land, looking like a war zone of felled tree soldiers, and took years of hard labor and help from Mother Nature to begin to remedy. Jim began clearing and digging a small 14 x 16 foot cellar hole by hand, hauling rocks that seemed to grow from the Wendell soil with each season, popping up like prairie dogs. The first beams were from hemlocks cut on the land and hand hewn. Jim started that winter in his 8' x 10' kitchen with one wall sheeted in plastic and an old metal Aubuchon stove with the stove pipe out a window. Soon enough he took refuge with a friend in Leverett for the winter, to start work again the following spring. When I came along the next year, the "Little House" had been erected and we began our life together. Our farm grew with chickens and with sheep in many shades of gray white, brown and black (Fairfield, Valentino, Natasha, Bo Diddley, Polka Pie to name a few) and for the first year or two our chunky, be-speckled gray, farm work-horse with the rather regal name of Gray Eagle, kept us warmer in winters with our dreams accompanied by the reassuring sounds of his breathing and munching while he stabled beneath us in the unfinished cellar. During this time Jim worked in restoring old houses and soon was building timber frames for others. His chisels and hand planes were sharpened and cared for with rever-ence. With our sheep flock expanding, I turned to spin-ning and weaving. There was usually a large galvanized bucket filled with water and curly wool soaking, prepar-ing to begin its (transformation /journey?) from cleaned fleece to carded roving and homespun yarn into blankets and rugs, sweaters and hats.

Music was a great form of entertainment and weekends were gathering times to sing and play music with friends. Wendell was home to a slew of bands so music was never far away.

Gardens were created and outbuildings sprouted as did our own family. We lived without electricity for 18 years with a hand pump at the kitchen sink and copper coils in the chimney to heat our bath water. Kerosene lamps and candles lit our home in warm light and bedtimes came early. This was a time of "back to the landers" and Wen-dell became the shelter for many young people who were trying to find a new way in the world.

Fifty years ago we were walking up a swampy dirt road to get home each day, an occasional frog leaping to the side out of permanent mud puddles; our young children in backpacks or trekking in gallantly holding our hands.

Now we can drive right up to the door, after years of added gravel and encroaching neighbors; their homes rising out of the woods with their own families and whose tribulations and loves and aspirations fill in the distance and the years and tether us more fully to a more contemporary world.

Old Egypt Homestead remains my retreat, however. That has not changed. Our little buildings fan out from the first small cottage to embrace transformations and new phases in our lives: a woodworking shop, Jim's spray laboratory, barn, house and even the remains of the outhouse. Below the outhouse, in our puddle of a pond, where once my sons had spent hours netting salamanders, leaping after frogs, and paddling in makeshift boats or rafts, now our visiting grandchildren troop down, with buckets and nets in hand, to continue these rituals of exploration.

Underfoot, it is easier to walk through the woods now, the trees larger, the understory not so dense, the slash from logging just before Jim first took up residence, mostly returned to the forest floor. Now it is my own body that makes the going more difficult; lifestyle changes, age, and arthritic joints limiting my woodland adventures, while still calling me into its magic and awe.

We live within walls, fashioned from trees like the ones that surround us and I am grateful. I thank them each day for their sacrifice to shelter us and sometimes to keep us warm when we assist the furnace by filling again the wood stove on cold winter nights. I thank them for the coolness of their shade on hot humid summer days. I thank them for their music as the breezes tickle their leaves. I thank them for giving homes to white-tailed deer, birds, chipmunks, the occasional bear, and even the porcupines with their disregard for our human industry and who remind us of our place in sharing this land.

I thank the forest for all the play forts that were constructed under their boughs by our sons and their friends. I thank them for sheltering the grave of my first-born.

I look up at the low ceiling in my kitchen/ dining area and see the slight smooth unevenness of the hand plane that I held so many years ago. I look at the corners of the room and see the hemlock timbers that Jim and I chiseled, a puzzle fit together with labor and sweat and love. I look out at the porch that my son Noah built and at the wide oak boards laid down by my son Seth, and by Jim. I look at the Rumford-designed fireplace with it's bricks that I had scrubbed clean of old lime and mortar from a Holyoke mill while pregnant with Noah, and that Jim and our friend, Nick, laid up with fireplaces, flues and arches to bring the dancing firelight into our home.

I also see the plaster wall has crumbled away in places, the corner by the stairs with pink insulation still peeking out, the section of floor that is sagging with joists that need to be replaced, the crack of light between the post and carrying beam in the kitchen because the final wall of outside sheathing has yet to be completed.

Our home continues to be a never ending project in process. It has been witness to bad times and good. Just as our life and all its stages, and changes continues to be a work in progress. We will die or perhaps have to move away first, and it will become someone else's process. But until then, Old Egypt Homestead remains our place of retreat and stewardship, an imperfect but loved sanctuary to shelter our imperfect but grateful, rich lives.

Jim and Phyllis (bottom right hand corner) gathering
with friends and instruments.

DORTHEE "DOR"

Interviewed by Ava Chiodo

"Wendell is a place where I could be out as a lesbian. There are people of different political persuasions getting along amicably. There were Wendell people against war. The forms it took for me were seven years of weekly silent vigil and being arrested five times demonstrating against Vermont Yankee."   - Dor

A Wendell Privy
By Dor

Maggie was digging the hole for my privy a rock at a time. After I went up to keep her company, pausing, she looked up, exclaiming "You mean you're not going to USE it!"

MAC (Maggie, Anne, & Chris) Construction had almost finished building my house. One day Anne announces that I better have a privy because I'm planning to move in without having been plumbed, not unusual at the time. I was among others exploring alternative sanitary systems. I tried a commercial compost toilet but the fan was too noisy in my 16'x24' space! Other arrangements worked for me and four years later I was plumbed.

Meanwhile there became a path going past the privy to Joanne's on Blueberry Lane. Initially staying in a trailer, she then had a crew building her house during which it was handy to use the privy!

It was also handy when Treechild in her non-toxic trailer stayed here and I became informed about being scent-free, because of others chemical sensitivity. She expressed gratitude for temporarily using the privy as a storage closet!

Recently, when Anna was working on the plans to build Kaymarion's house here, she requested use of the privy for construction workers. Good idea, but it needed some repairs. She rehung the door; Sarah and Mark replaced the rotten ventilation portal.

Again serviceable. Yay!

Dor's Portrait
painted by Paula Gottlieb

JONATHAN von RANSON

Interviewed by Luke Chiodo

"I am surrounded by plants, animals and fellow humans all doing their best, including the humans, to live a good life and enable it for others. The people have a deeper than ordinary sense of relationship, and connection to life in its all togetherness." - Jonathan

A Night in the Wendell Woods
By Jonathan von Ranson

I was born in New York City but raised from age four in rural Connecticut. All together, it made me more of a country boy than a city one...except for being afraid of the woods at night. During the day, the woods were our neighborhood playground. But...well, if it was after dark, I remember galloping the three hundred yards home from my cousin's as if yellow-eyed wolves were growling at my heels.

Once married, in newspaper work and settled into a neighborhood of tiny plots in West Hartford, I found myself longing for some real land to love again. A classified ad appeared in the Hartford Courant for "72 acres, Wendell, Mass., $8,000." So I...copped out. "Just a crazy fantasy," I told myself, "plus, at $110 an acre, that's already sold, for sure."

But a friend who knew of my dream spotted the ad and asked if I'd seen it. She encouraged me to call the seller. I did – and there'd been no sale yet. Jack, the owner, offered to take my then-wife and me to visit it.

This property was virtually inaccessible. The car inched over roots and stones to within a quarter mile, then we walked.

It was forestland in some serious terrain: a high ridge running east-west with a steep drop-off to the north. To the south lay a vale with a line of cliffs, a tiny stream and – intriguingly – a boulder pile that looked still freshly spewed out by the last glacier. The slash of an aborted logging job added a certain twist and tangle. All this enticement two miles from from any maintained road! I was smitten.

Jack decided he only wanted to let go of 60 acres, for $7,000, which was OK with me. After calling my parents and grandparents and convincing them to lend us the money, I drove to Jack's house in Middletown and signed.

But within days he called to inform me another offer had been made – before mine. A New York buyer had signed with a New York agent. He apologized that our deal was off. That seemed to spell the end, but on a lawyer-friend's advice, I wrote Jack a letter saying I was honoring our purchase-and-sale agreement and expecting still to close.

A suspenseful month went by, then came the news that we could complete the purchase!

Twice, friends' encouragement had revived my pursuit of this "impossible" dream. Once we owned the land, every few weeks we'd escape West Hartford, where I edited the West Hartford News, and come up – my first wife, Brooks, Erik, Kristin, Joel and me – and camp for the weekend. We'd set up near the cliffs and boulders, which the kids loved to climb. Joel was well up into a small tree, once, before he noticed a porcupine inches above him.

One late afternoon, a couple of months after the purchase, it hit me to do a solo overnight on the land. I drove up and came in from the north. You had to cross the Millers on the rickety, condemned bridge in Erving Center (damaged, I learned later, by the truckloads of logs from our land), then turn right and drive along the river to where a badly eroded logging trail headed up the mountain to the left. The VW Microbus could somehow handle it all, and this evening it scrambled right up to the old cellar hole.

That foundation supported the house where Jesse and Mary Fisher had homesteaded until Jesse died in 1817 – the year following the "Year without a Summer," a year in which there was frost every month. Dust from a tremendous volcanic explosion in the Pacific had dimmed the planet's sunlight throughout 1816. Crops had failed. From the probate records of this indebted dirt farmer, it appears that the extra burden spelled his end. The court settled the estate by giving Mary her "Widow Fisher's Thirds" (a third of the parcel) and the southeast room of the house that had stood next to where I was parked.

It was nightfall. I struck off crosslots for the ridge, a bag of provisions in hand and a sleeping bag tucked under my arm. I had only a vague sense of the terrain, and the underbrush became dense and springy. I fought through it with mounting anxiety. Would I get lost? Would I impale my eye on a branch in the failing light? What opportunistic denizens were tracking my half-panicked movements? I loved this land, but would that triumph?

Heart pounding, I miraculously found the ridge and the tiny clearing I'd been aiming for. It was early night. Seated on a low rock, the Millers River Valley spread steeply below me and Bear Mountain with its still largely unexplored cleft at my back, I ate my supper out of a paper bag, suppressing the bag's crinkling noises.

Then it was time for the real test. I unrolled my sleeping bag on a nearby bed of soft moss, took off my shoes and climbed in, fully dressed. *OK, a little cozy, maybe, but hardly secure.* My breaths were shallow.

The Big Dipper began to shine in the patch of northern sky above my clearing. I lay there taking in the darkening heavens but distracted by what might be approaching from the woods. A couple of hours went by. Meteorites arced and stars and planes twinkled far above. Leaves rustled, owls hooted and twigs snapped.

Jonathan on Bear Mountain

The sky was so deep. The valley before me was so vast. Pride and awe were making inroads. With six years as a newspaper editor behind me, I thought to ask, *What headlines have I ever read about attacks by predatory animals, depraved mountain men, etc. on campers* in Western New England? I couldn't recall any...

I slept, waking a few times to see the Big Dipper rotated a little further around the North Star and realizing a wonderful new comfortableness in the woods at night.

SUSAN von RANSON

Interviewed by Sally Houle

"My life in Wendell has been some hard work - gardening, wood splitting - great company in my husband (Jonathan), good friends and good walks...It lets me be myself, dress simply, and walk safely." -Susan

Nearer to Friends
By Susan von Ranson

I came to Wendell in 1980 moving from NJ to join Jonathan in his cabin deep in the forest. He had chosen to live without the modern amenities, building a small stone house, and gardening for our food. Sometimes Wendell friends made the rough two-mile trip in to see us, but through the years we missed an easier way to participate in our wonderful community and to be nearer to friends.

In 1996 we sold our woodland home, and moved to an old farmhouse right on the main street in the center of the town. We were already part of the community in many ways, and enjoyed our new closeness to our friends.

One cool morning in late November of 2012, I went out to the backyard clothesline carrying a rather heavy basket of washed clothes. For this quick job, I skipped changing to my boots and went without a coat. To set the scene, the clothesline sits down a wee slope from the front yard, and there was a very light layer of snow sprinkled between the blades of grass.

Sure enough, being in a hurry in the cool wind, I slipped, my right leg shot out in front of me, I leaned back and – still holding the heavy laundry – was thrown down into a hard sitting position smack onto my left leg, bent at the knee. Crack! Crack! I knew I had broken my lower leg.

Feeling I'd been careless and now unable to move, my first worry was that Jonathan was not at home. He'd gone to the YMCA in Athol. I was in trouble and increasing pain, and far enough from the road that yelling would not work. How to get help? My only phone (a land-line) was in the house many yards away. "I know, I'll wave down someone in a car!" I thought, though not many, cars pass our house regularly.

I waved, thrusting my arm back and forth, an expression of agony on my face. What I got was several people happily waving back and driving on. "What can I do??? What's a signal that I need help???" I was dragging my now terribly pained and crooked-legged self closer to the road. "I know, palms of hands together, eyes to the sky, PRAY!" The next vehicle, a van, stopped immediately.

Well, I had come to the right town. Paul, the son of an old Wendell family, came quicky to the rescue asking "Where is Jonathan? OK, do you want to go to to the hospital? Greenfield or Athol? Do you want me to call for an ambulance or take you in the van? The van? Mike!" (his friend who was with him), "Clear out the back." Paul called the YMCA and the hospital. He grabbed the long couch cushion and some pillows from the living room, threw them into the emptied van, and he and Mike carried and settled me in for the ride to Athol. I swear all this happened in less than 9 minutes.

Both the tibia and fibula bones were broken, and I began a long healing process with casts and a rod. I was first in a bed that Jonathan brought downstairs, then in a wheelchair, then crutches, and neighbors and friends brought us dinner meals for many many weeks.

Our move gave us the closeness and friendships we will always be thankful for.

Susan Churning Butter

Susan and Jonathan

45

NANCY SPITTLE

Interviewed by Hannah Dziedzic

""I'm happy with living in the woods, in close community, in a well-run small town atmosphere with lots of things to do. It's given me space to breathe, to build on my dreams."
  -Nancy

My Memorable Wendell Experience
By Nancy Spittle

I came to Wendell in 1977 with a vision, like many who arrived in the 70's, of getting a piece of land, build my own little house and have a small homestead scene. Friend Rick Drohen first found land here in 1972- cheap! $6000 for a 55 acre back lot that had been recently logged and left rough. He got a 4 WD truck that could handle the logging road access, bought a little 10 ft square cabin with a pyramid glassed roof and sleeping loft, and set it up on posts.

Rick had another friend who wanted to homestead and split the land with Rick, each retaining their own 2 acre building lot and sharing the rest. This friend John lived in a 32' mobile home with attached stick-built living room added on; but he eventually decided he'd rather buy a house more centrally located than build in Wendell. Rick offered me and another friend to buy out John's half, and I moved into John's mobile home, at the site of Rick's present workshop. Some other friends also found land next to us (Tom Mangan and Jean Forward) or across the street (Steve Gross and Diane Kurinsky) and were building their homes. I bought into the property in 1978.

Our relationship continued to grow and we decided to have a child- Gabriel, born in 1979. Rick added an addition onto the half- saltbox type house he had been building since '73 to create two more bedrooms and a larger living space. In my last month of pregnancy with Gabriel, Tom and Jean had a house raising, where a couple dozen of us got together to raise the post and beam frame for their 3 story house. They lived in a mobile home with their 2 year old son while they were building, and Jean was pregnant again. Diane and Steve had hired Jim Slavas to construct their post and beam house across the street, which he laboriously did with all hand tools, while listening to classical music. Diane was also pregnant.

We chose to have a home birth, in true homesteader fashion, but certified midwives were not allowed to practice independently or in homes in Massachusetts then, so we went to Westminster VT to deliver our son at the midwife's home. Within a few months, Shoshana Gross and Caleb Keller were delivered by the same midwife, so we say these 3 schoolmates were "born in the same bed". Gabriel Drohen, Shoshi Gross, Jesse Mangan and Caleb Keller were in the same class through Swift River.

Diane and Jean were both working on doctoral degrees when these kids were born, and I was a working RN following a 4 month maternity leave. After sharing our pregnancies and building our "nests" so intimately and living so close to each other, we began to share in the care of each other's babies. Each of us agreed to take all the kids one day a week, giving each mother 2 "free" days, dramatically cutting childcare costs. That one day a week was hard work, starting with eating a huge breakfast and pounding fluids all day to be able to nurse 3 infants! And of course the diaper scene, or dressing all to go outdoors in cold weather was wild. We shared colds and chicken pox.

I have great respect for any mother of triplets. The kids thrived on the regular time with age mates, and young Tom Mangan got to play the big brother role for all three when he was also included during non school days. I used to bundle all 3 toddlers into a wagon and trudge them up our dirt driveway and along the road to the center of town so they could play at the playground. Later, that playground was their preschool site before it was rebuilt into our beautiful Wendell library.

The kids called the other parents "Aunty Dee" or "Mama Jean" and as they grew older, we would help with sports and lessons transportation, back up each other for calls from the school nurse, and even take each other's kids for a weekend so one couple could have an adult getaway weekend. This arrangement continued when Mara Gross was born in 1982 and Brianna in 1983, both here in their

Wendell homes, as our Vermont midwife had retired and passed her practice to a lay midwife who came to our homes. Then there were six kids on each mom's day.

I am so grateful to have lived in a place where we have such community. These women who I shared infant care and child rearing with were already trusted friends, and we were in a similar phase of life. The roots we established run deep. All of us still live in the same homes. Most years, Diane and Steve have us over for Hanukkah and Passover and we have them for Christmas and Easter. We had to stop celebrating Thanksgiving together as their family grew with 3 children's partners, grandkids, and in-laws. We still walk together, often vacation together and honor each other's birthdays. We call on each other when car or household mishaps occur or when to share dinner on our garden patios. These women and other friends had a standing Friday evening mom's happy hour for over thirty years, where none of us cooked; we just brought healthy finger foods and everyone helped themselves to food and visited while the kids played and moms had a glass or two of wine.

It has also been such a great gift to live in the same place and so close to nature for over 40 years now, after living in 15 places in my first 30 years. The wildlife and environment changes: there are fewer birds, frogs and racoons now, but more bears and turkeys. The growing season is longer. There seem to be fewer days of good snow for cross country skiing.

Nancy and Rick's new house under construction.

RICK DROHEN

Interviewed by Zachary Serrell

"If a town could have a soul, Wendell has one."
-Rick

An Odyssey into Home, Friends and Community
By Rick Drohen

It started when I was nine years old. I was being raised by a single mother in the Northeast Kingdom in Newport, Vermont, 16 miles from the Canadian border. All my aunts and uncles were either loggers or farmers. By necessity they would help each other out fostering a feeling of caring. Folks would get together for hay harvesting and barn building. When people got married or died the community would make food to share. This goodness was imprinted on me like a trout. It's what gave me a sense of a social community, a network. I grew up with that feeling of belonging.

When I was 16, we moved to Haverhill because my mom remarried. It was like going to a different world; it felt safe and like I was on an adventure. The rest of my childhood was spent growing up in Haverhill. After that, I went on to become an Army Medic.

After the army I went to Essex Community College and then transferred to UMASS. Because I had been a soldier I did not have to live on campus. I was blessed to find a group of people who became my community and surrogate family. We would go on road trips, travel through different towns. When driving through Wendell, I thought this is the kind of town I want to live in.

As my time at UMass ended, all my friends left on adventures. I had decided I would go to India, but I needed a place for my things and a place to come back to. Having grown up with loggers I went around to sawmills to ask about land because in those days, loggers would buy lots, timber them and sell off the property. I met Steve Clark of Warwick and he had several lots he had or was logging.

It was on a rainy nasty day that I met Steve here on this land. Even though it had piles of brush and limbs and it was raining this land somehow felt like home. I thought, "This is my spot!" It cost $6,000 I didn't have, but I knew someone who did. That friend lent me $3,000 for the down payment and Steve's friend, Audrey Greenwald offered me a job so I could pay off the balance. I invited my friends to buy into the land when they returned from their travels.

I found a 12' x 12' cabin with a pyramid roof and a gorgeous door for sale in North Leverett for $150. My friend Joe lent me his bulldozer and his flat bed truck to move the cabin. We took the roof off and rolled it onto the flat bed. It was like watching the crusades, men and ropes hoisting the cabin onto the truck. The Leverett Police stopped us, asked us what we were doing and then gave us an escort!

Dan Trenholm put in a driveway and I got the cabin set up complete with a hanging bed, as the space was so small. I lived there with my dog, Joshua. To get electricity to the cabin I had to call the electric company every week for eight weeks. Each week they would put in one more pole. The cost of an electric pole in the early 1970's was $50.00 a pole.

When I started building my house, I invited my friends to come live on the land. Warren Oliver moved a trailer for us and my friend John Dunphy moved into that trailer. "Warnie" Oliver dug me a trench with his backhoe and we put in an out-house. However, it was too close in the summer and too far in the winter! Rupert Goddard came and dowsed the well.

I remember when Jack Ellis pulled a truck out for me. He was a sweetheart. His brother, Donnie Ellis was a horse trader. Donnie told me, " If you make a dollar more than you spend in a day you'll be a rich man."

At that time a lot of hippies were coming to town. Wendell had so many bands back then, it seemed like there was a band on every block! There was also a strong women's community.

Nancy (Spittle) who I married years later, moved onto the land around 1976. Steve Gross put a trailer on the land and soon after Diane Kurinsky bought a house in Wendell and then the land across the road from us. Our friends Jean Forward and Tom Mangan bought and lived on the 66 acres next door.

Diane, Jean, and our friend Annelise all got their PHD's that year. They also all had babies the same year Nancy and I had our first baby, Gabriel. The women would get together every Friday night so they could talk to someone who would give them more than a one syllable response! They named themselves The Get Along Gang and after many decades get together still.

I remember events like the annual Halloween party that was put on by the Ladies Aide Society. A great memory is of a Halloween party at Michael and Karen Idoine's on John Quist Road. There were four fire circles and another one in the middle. The fires signified Earth, Fire, Water and Air. We were given a crystal and sang a song together. I remember Mark Stewart dancing. It was magical. We weren't even high.

Then The Full Moon Coffee House started up to fund the Save Bear Mountain effort to stop the state from rerouting Route 2 through Bear Mountain. A lot of great musicians as well as the unique came to perform. There was one guy who got up on the stage for the open mic who played the Star Spangled Banner on a cow bell. The audience listened and then shouted out, "Play Ball!" The Full Moon Coffee House still operates today.

I remember at Town Meetings back then the hippies would sit on the right side of the town hall and the conservatives would sit on the left. But as years went on and people intermingled, we all started sitting together. At that time Ted Lewis was a selectman flanked by two gay women on the board. I remember someone saying it's not what you look like but what you put into it. I did my part by serving on the Highway Commission in the 1980's. Here in Wendell we attend to each other.

Back then I worked as a psych nurse and would be so happy to come home to Wendell.

Rick and Nancy's new home being built next to Rick's small cabin

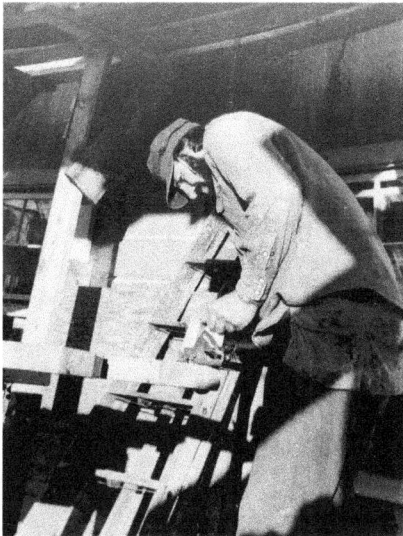

Rick working on the new house.

"Your house is who you are." Rick

CHRISTINE HEARD

Interviewed by Zachary Serrell

"I am very happy in Wendell. I love the friendly, caring community of people and the beautiful, natural landscape." - Christine

Fiske Pond Becomes Town Property
by Christine Heard

Not long after I arrived in Wendell in the fall of 1977, I realized an important trait prevalent in our townspeople ... tolerance. Citizens of Wendell varied greatly in age, education, jobs, family size and configuration and, most important, in their viewpoints. But I found most people tolerated and still do tolerate those who are different from them. People from different backgrounds enjoy getting to know one another and working together to accomplish what Wendell wanted and needed.

For more than 22 years I served on the Wendell Selectboard here in Wendell. I loved being on the Wendell Selectboard. The work was interesting; my colleagues were agreeable and hardworking; the caliber of most town officials was superb, intelligent, open minded, hardworking and cooperative. Our cooperative and thoughtful approach resulted in Selectboard decisions that were mostly by consensus ... a rare and valuable trait in town government.

In 2004 the Fiske Pond property had been owned by Chickadees, Inc. for several years. The organization was unable to sustain the property and so offered to sell it to the Town. Many citizens were excited to protect the property and keep it open as a family swimming hole which it had been for many years. It seemed like a wonderful opportunity to many.

At this time the Selectboard members were Ted Lewis, Dan Keller and me. We depended on our Finance Committee for good advice on all fiscal matters. The FinCom was not in favor of the Town's purchasing the property mostly because taxes are not collected on town property; owning Fiske Pond would further reduce the tax base. In this matter Ted, Dan and I agreed that it was important to keep as much property as possible on the tax rolls. In addition to the loss of taxes, managing the property would cost the Town more money for upkeep, etc. Also, Wendell was already discussing and planning for construction of a new library and a new town office building, big expenses to come with an increase in taxes.

After some research I discovered that one third of land in Wendell was owned by the Commonwealth as State Forest or as Fish and Wildlife Conservation Areas. Another one third of our land was also removed from the tax rolls (mostly owned by Mass Audubon) or was in Chapter 61, i.e., privately owned woodlands managed for tree growth and wildlife habitat in exchange for a lower tax rate. That left only one third of our land (about 900 citizens, which included children) available for regular taxation, to pay for roads, schools, and other town government functions. Further reductions to our tax base seemed unwise.

Wendell citizens presented their views to us frequently but always politely and kindly ... part of that tolerance I mentioned earlier. As 2004 wound down, we seemed at an impasse. Fortunately, there was a town election planned in January 2005. The Selectboard put a non-binding referendum article on the ballot asking whether townsfolk wished to purchase and own the Fiske Pond property. The ballot vote was resoundingly in favor of the purchase. The Selectboard accepted the townspeople's vote without discussion and turned our energies to direction from the townsfolk.

Although I was against the purchase, I have come to enjoy Fiske Pond tremendously. I am proud that our citizens had the foresight to buy it and create a clean, pretty swimming spot and wonderful trails for walking people and dogs. Fiske Pond gets a great deal of use mostly by townspeople, but others too enjoy it. It's a delightful part of Wendell where people share the landscape with each other, with other creatures and practice tolerance and acceptance for all.

Fiske Pond

WILLIAM "BOO" PEARSON

Interviewed by Hannah Dziedzic

"My life in Wendell is bordering on the unbelievable - certainly extraordinary...and always enriched by the influences of others I met here and lived and worked with. Wendell has a richness of its community members' diverse abilities and how they combine to act harmoniously. Also, the richness of its many eco-niches, its relative remoteness, elevation, and space." - Boo

Wendell
By William "Boo" Pearson

Boo on Loose Caboose Stage 1978

By 1978 the nucleus of the Loose Caboose was in residence at # 19 Locke Village Road, with Harry & Del Williston's place next door to the north and Janet Mankowsky's small farm on the opposite, southern side of our home. It was busy there.

We rehearsed frequently in the basement, the spot where our equipment and instruments were stored. Just beyond the top of the basement stairs was a small office where bookings were made by phone and the band's accounts were kept. On the wall above a desk were co-joined highway maps of New England, a bright red pin designating Wendell's location with hand drawn, co-centric circles penciled in, emanating outwards from Wendell intervals of 50 miles.

We were busy finding work and mapping our route to World Domination.

Every Monday night we'd meet for marathon business meetings in the living room. Discussions and debates were wide-ranging but focused on the improvement of our status vis-a-vis the broader pop music scene. We were a self avowed reggae band and reggae was foreign and new to Americans in the 1970's.

We hustled to generate gigs and keep touring. We owned a raft of original material we hoped to record.

As a result of the collective push forward, I volunteered to organize a monthly mail out, a list of upcoming shows to be sent to our growing fan base for promotional purposes. It seemed like a good idea; other bands were making similar efforts with good effect. But it was a lot of work to put together and maintain. There were hundreds of envelopes to send out in a timely fashion and each needed a stamp. The first few mail outs were expensive and the cost of the project soon became prohibitive.

The Loose Caboose band needed to obtain a Bulk Mailing Stamp from the United States Postal Service if we were to be able to afford sending out our monthly calendar of performances.

There was one person in Wendell to speak with and discuss the issue: Wendell's Postmistress, Gladys Powling. Luckily, Merle and Gladys Powling lived directly across the street from the band's place at #19 Locke Village Road. Their cows were pastured there in a field surrounded by a fence and a small grove of apple trees.

There was a working telephone booth in front of their home, 20 feet away from the stop sign at the far corner of their front yard.

A lot of folks spent 25 cents a pop to use that phone, but everyone in Wendell used the Powling's front porch, the place where Gladys over saw the collection and distribution of the town's mail.

Gladys was enthusiastic when I approached her with a request to purchase a Bulk Mailing Stamp. She claimed that it was the first ever issued to a Wendell resident and that its sale would place her in a better paid "category" when she collected compensatory checks from the U.S. Postal Service upon the occasion of her retirement.

She was so pleased that she offered to bake an apple pie for the band. Everyone knew she could cook.
How was I to refuse?

She dismissed my offer to pick up enough fallen apples from beneath the trees near the cow pasture, and called for Merle.

Together we stepped off her front porch and stood beneath a 30 foot tall apple tree as Merle climbed to its top. He, too, rebuffed my offers to help.

Standing in a notch near the tree top, Merle grabbed a large branch in either hand and, arms and legs akimbo, shook the apple tree for all he was worth. Ripe apples rained down on the Powling's lawn.

The cows noticed and ambled towards us. Laughing, Merle said that the herd would be drunk that night.

The apple pie baked and gifted by Gladys Powling was scrumptious and quickly consumed. Perhaps I should have kept it a secret and eaten it all myself.

But we shared everything we had back in 1978. I remember thinking that I wanted to be able to climb to the top of apple trees and shake down the fruit when I was a septuagenerian like Merle was then.

I'm working on that one.

Boo and Ras Jahn (Loose Caboose Percussionist)

ANNE DIEMAND BUCCI
"ANNIE"

Interviewed by Matthew Regnier

"Anything I wanted to do in the Town of Wendell, I had the full support of whomever happened to be in charge."
  -Annie

The Diemand Family gets their Polio Vaccine.

My Life in Wendell
By Annie Diemand Bucci

I was the eleventh child of twelve children born to a large working farm family on Mormon Hollow Road. I was named Anne after St. Anne's School in Turners Falls which is where I attended grammar school.
I have so many fond memories of growing up on Diemand Egg Farm.

When I was a kid most of the roads in Wendell were dirt, including the one in front of the farm. As well as raising thousands of chickens, first for meat, then for eggs, we had yellow ducks that lived in a barn behind the farm house. The ducks would cross the road as there was a pond on the other side. I remember cars driving so slow that they would stop and let the ducks cross.

My first memory of working on the farm was in the early 1960's. In the space where our kitchen and store are now is where we dressed the chickens then. I was four or five years old and would stand on a pail next to my mom. She would cut and clean the chickens and I would then clean the gizzards out. You had to be strong enough to pull out that membrane, it wasn't easy.

The coolest thing was I would find really pretty stones and even pennies in the gizzards!

Back then a penny bought penny candy!
I have fond memories of my mother. I remember her being patient with me. I remember her taking out the fine china and polishing the silver for the holidays.

When I was young and in grade school I would collect the eggs although I was too little to carry a basket. I remember my brothers carried the wire baskets which got pretty heavy when filled with eggs.

My first taste of Wendell was going to Mahar in seventh grade. It was my first time on a school bus! If our family went anywhere together we would all pile into my parent's station wagon.

I remember going up to the two-room schoolhouse to take an aptitude test. It was where our current library is now. That's where I met Cheryl Prim, Geneva Hildreth and Anita Wing. We became friends.

I also have fond memories of joining the Wendell Fire Department. At nineteen years old I was looking for something more in my life. I served on the Fire Department for 14 years. Roland Jean was the Fire Chief back then with Everett Ricketts as the Assistant Fire Chief. When Everett became Chief, Harry Williston became the Assistant Fire Chief. Bob Bowers was the Captain and I was the Lieutenant.

Vic Coy, my brother Peter and his wife Linda, as well as my sister Faith and her husband Al MacIntyre also served on the Fire Department back then. The Fire Station was the building next to the Wendell Town Hall in those days.

I have a great memory from the 1970's of the guys in the Outer Space Band jumping on the fire truck, and helping to pull out the hoses. They lived on the corner next to what now is our Wendell Free Library. The guys in the band were Klondike Koehler, Johnny Moses, Elliot Osbourne and Dave Robinson.

I have also served on the Ladies Aide Committee, the Wendell Recreation Commission and worked on the Wendell Post. I started The Friends of the Wendell Free Library when one of the Golden Agers died and donations were coming in. Marion Herrick was a Library Trustee then.

When Anne Zak was a selectman she asked me to join the Wendell Police Department because they needed more diversity. At this time it was an all male Police Department.
I told Police Chief Ed Chase I wanted to be a "peace officer." I had met Ed through Tilly Burnett. Jay Blackbird and his son Cain Blackbird were also serving on the Police Department.
I had a wonderful relationship with Ed. He was steady, knowledgeable, strong and caring. I served on the Wendell Police Department for 29 years.

One of my greatest pleasures was to be Ed Chase's co-worker and friend.

WENDELL POLICE
DEPARTMENT

This certifies that

Ann E. Diemand

is an officer of this
department

DATE   POLICE CHIEF

OFFICER'S SIGNATURE

I am currently the appointed Constable in Wendell.

Ed Chase, Annie, Ted Lewis, Christine Heard

ACKNOWLEDGEMENTS

Many thanks to the people who have supported and participated in the making of Faces of Wendell.

New Salem Academy Grant

Wendell Cultural Council

Friends of the Wendell Free Library

Wendell Free Library

Nathan Scheele for editing and formatting DVDs of the teen interviews.

Paul Richmond, Human Error Publishing

Genevieve Gaignard for her gift of Photography

Pamela A. Richardson for her heart felt review.

Richie Davis for his kind review and editing with encouraging feedback.

Johanna Bartlett for editing

Cody Vanhoutte - Faces of Wendell Website designer and administrator.

Teens: Ava Chiodo, Luke Chiodo, Hannah Dziedzic, Sally Houle, Zachary Serrell

Special thanks to the Wendell teens who spent many Saturday mornings working on their interview questions, interviewing and recording their seniors, and preparing for the town presentation at the Wendell Free Library which was a smashing success thanks to their hard work.

Ava Chiodo

Hannah Dziedzic

Luke Chiodo

Matt Regnier

Sally Houle

Zachary Serrell

DVD's of the complete teen interviews may be purchased for $10 at The Wendell Country Store, Diemand Egg Farm, and The New Salem Country Store.

To contact us:

Faces of Wendell
P.O. Box 212
Wendell, MA. 01379

FacesofWendell@gmail.com

To read more Wendell Stories or to submit your own, visit our website.

FacesofWendell.com

www.ingramcontent.com/pod-product-compliance
Lightning Source LLC
Chambersburg PA
CBHW072013060426
42446CB00043B/2424